PRAYERS AND GRACES

COLLECTED BY
ALLAN M. LAING

WITH ILLUSTRATIONS BY
MERVYN PEAKE

PRAYERS AND GRACES

A LITTLE BOOK
OF EXTRAORDINARY PIETY

PAN BOOKS
LONDON AND SYDNEY

First published by Victor Gollancz Ltd
as *Prayers and Graces* in 1944 and
More Prayers and Graces in 1957
This edition published 1981 by Pan Books Ltd,
Cavaye Place, London sw10 9pg
© Allan M. Laing and Mervyn Peake 1944 & 1957
isbn 0 330 26533 4
Printed in Great Britain by
Richard Clay (The Chaucer Press) Ltd, Bungay, Suffolk

CONTENTS

Book 2

ACKNOWLEDGEMENTS

For permission to reprint copyright material, my grateful thanks are due to Mr. Hesketh Pearson (for an extract from *Skye High*); to the Exors. of the late John Sampson, the publishers, Messrs. Chatto and Windus, and the translator (for "Prayer of the Gipsy Modoran" and "Prayer of a Romany Rye" from *The Wind on the Heath*. I have taken the liberty of partly re-writing the second poem); to the Editor of *The Countryman* (for "Crisis in the Nursery"); to Messrs. George Allen and Unwin (for "A Benison on Wartime High Tea," from my own *Bank Holiday on Parnassus*); to the Editor of the *New Statesman and Nation* (for "A Common Grace"); and to Mr. Alasdair Alpin MacGregor (for an extract from *Auld Reekie: Portrait of a Lowland Boyhood*).

I have also to thank Mr. Raymond Mortimer and Professor Graham A. Laing of Pasadena for acquainting me with, respectively, "Nursery Limerick" and "Anecdote for God."

Kind permission for the use of copyright material (for which I am duly grateful) has been granted by Messrs. George Allen & Unwin, Ltd. (for J. M. Synge's poem, *The Curse*); Messrs. Jonathan Cape, Ltd. and the Exors. of Samuel Butler (for a prayer from *Samuel Butler's Notebooks*); Messrs. Robert Hale, Ltd. (for a passage from Fred Gresswell's *Bright Boots*); and "Harley Quinn" (for the *Prayer of a Property Profiteer*). In several cases I have been unable to make contact with copyright owners, and I hope they will forgive me for taking permission for granted.

I take the opportunity here to thank correspondents who very kindly sent me further examples of "extraordinary piety"; and I much regret my inability to include more than a few of them herein.

A. M. L.

PRAYERS AND GRACES

THE BABY'S GRACE

Praise to God who giveth meat
Convenient unto all who eat:
Praise for tea and buttered toast,
Father, Son and Holy Ghost.

R. L. GALES

A GIPSY BABE'S PRAYER

Little bird of Sparadise,
Do the work of Jesus Chrise:
Go by sea: go by lan':
Go by Goddes holy han'.

PATIENCE DAVIS, *a gipsy*

TOO MUCH RABBIT

For rabbits young and rabbits old,
For rabbits hot and rabbits cold,
For rabbits tender, rabbits tough,
We thank Thee, Lord: we've had enough.

Attributed to DEAN SWIFT

THIS PRAYER BUSINESS

Then Miss Watson she took me in the closet and prayed, but nothing come of it. She told me to pray every day, and whatever I asked for I would get it. But it warn't so. I tried it. Once I got a fish-line, but no hooks. It warn't any good to me without hooks. I tried for the hooks three or four times, but somehow I couldn't make it work. I asked Miss Watson to try for me, but she said I was a fool. She never told me why, and I couldn't make it out no way.

MARK TWAIN

RECIPROCITY

Here lie I, Martin Elginbrodde:
Hae mercy o' my soul, Lord God,
As I would do, were I Lord God
And Ye were Martin Elginbrodde.

EPITAPH IN ELGIN CATHEDRAL

STRANGE PETITION

Hesketh Pearson, joint author with Hugh Kingsmill of *Skye High*, woke up one morning to find himself muttering:

"We earnestly pray Almighty God to persuade the municipal council to give us another poet like Shelley, if he can be spared from the freedom of the seas."

THE ANGLER'S PRAYER

Give me, O Lord, to catch a fish
  So large that even I,
In boasting of it afterwards,
  Shall have no need to lie.

ANON

COAXING THE DEITY

'O Lord, Thou knowest we are about to have a little bazaar. . . .'

LATE TRADITIONAL

PRAYER OF THE GIPSY MODORAN

Sweet little God, I beseech thee to grant me everything I ask, because thou art beautiful, high and mighty.

If thou lettest me steal a loaf, brandy, a hen, a goose, a pig or a horse, I will give thee a big candle.

If I have stolen anything, and the Gentiles enter my tent to discover the stolen property, and find nothing, I will give thee two big candles.

If the officers of the law enter my tent, and having searched it and found nothing, depart in peace, I will give thee three big candles.

Because thou art my sweet little golden God.

FROM THE RUMANIAN

THE CHOSEN GIVE THANKS

Some hae meat, and canna eat,
　　And some wad eat that want it;
But we hae meat, an' we can eat,
　　And sae the Lord be thankit.

ROBERT BURNS

YOU CAN'T PLEASE EVERYBODY

The Duke of Rutland urged *The Times* to pray
For rain: the rain came down the following day.
The pious marvelled: sceptics murmured: "Fluke!"
And farmers late with hay said: "Damn that Duke!"

Quoted by E. V. LUCAS

REBUKE FOR JONES

"For what we are about to receive, and for what
Mr. Jones has already received, may the Lord make
us truly thankful. Amen."

ANON

MIRACLE WANTED

O Lord, who made these loaves and fishes,
Look down upon these two poor dishes
And, though they be exceeding small,
Make them enough, we pray, for all;
For if they should our stomachs fill,
Heaven will have wrought a miracle.

ANON

PRAYER FOR THE PIOUS

Buried in earth or drown'd in th' main,
 Eat up by worms or fishes,
I pray the pious may obtain
 For happy times, their wishes.

THOMAS FULLER

NO PRAYER FROM THE SCOFFER

Though to the Mosque I come with pious air,
By Allah! think not that I come for prayer;
  I stole a mat once, from a worshipper:
That sin worn out, again I here repair.

OMAR KHAYYAM

HARVEST THANKSGIVING

"O Lord, we thank Thee for the abundance and safe in-gathering of all our harvest except for a few fields between here and Stonehaven. . . ."

Quoted by DEAN RAMSAY

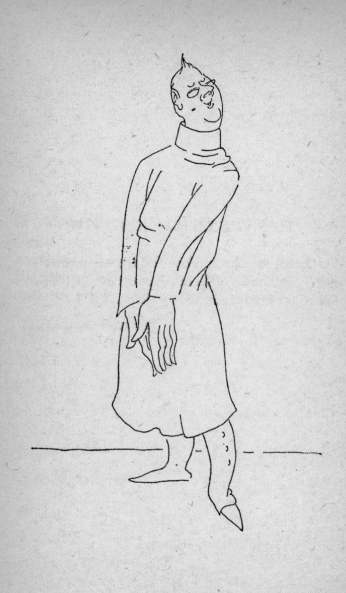

AN ANECDOTE FOR GOD

A curate, having taken considerable trouble to prepare a speech for a public meeting, found himself, to his disgust, called upon only to lead the audience in prayer. Determined not to waste his material, he embodied most of his speech in his prayer, one passage of which ran:

"Lest this point be too obscure, O Lord, permit Thy servant to illustrate it with an anecdote. . . ."

THE SERVANT MAID'S PRAYER

"O Lord, have I got to get up?"

CRISIS IN THE NURSERY

"Dear Satan, please come for Nurse, and please come soon."

A PARSON-POLITICIAN PRAYS

"O Lord, we ask Thee for a Governor who would rule in the fear of God; who would defeat the ringleaders of corruption, enhance the prosperity of the State, promote the happiness of the people—O Lord, what's the use of beating about the bush? Give us George W. Briggs for Governor! Amen."

FATHER TAYLOR

GENERAL MONTGOMERY GIVES THANKS

"We must not forget to give thanks to the Lord, 'mighty in battle,' for giving us such a good beginning towards the attainment of our object. . . .

"And now let us get on with the job. Together with our American Allies, we have knocked Mussolini off his perch. We will now drive the Germans from Sicily."

DAILY PRESS (1943)

COME, LET US BARGAIN WITH THE LORD

"Lord, give us grace, for if Thou give us not grace, we shall not give Thee glory; and who will win by that, Lord?"

THE REV. MR. HOUSTON

A BENISON ON WARTIME HIGH TEA

Upon this scanty meal, O Lord,
Bestow a blessing in accord:
Pour Thy grace in measure small,
Lest it more than cover all.

Bless the tiny piece of ham:
Bless the lonely dab of jam:
Bless the sparsely-buttered toast,
Father, Son and Holy Ghost.

A. M. L.

GRADUATED GRATITUDE

Bishop Wilberforce used to tell the story of a greedy
clergyman who, when asked to say grace, would
look anxiously to see if there were champagne
glasses on the table. If there were, he would begin:
"O most bountiful Jehovah!..."; but if he saw only
claret glasses, he would pray: 'We are not worthy,
O Lord, of these, the least of Thy mercies...."

PRAYER OF A ROMANY RYE

O my God, to still my longing,
　Give to me a mantle fine,
Gaily trimmed with metal buttons
　In the golden light to shine.

Grant me, too, a goodly wife,
　In her jacket, clean and neat,
Arms of slender willow grace,
　Flowerlike beauty in her feet.

Laughing eyes, like seed of grape,
　Shapely shoulders, like white bread,
Lips as fresh as buds that burst
　Into shining blossoms red.

TRANSYLVANIAN GIPSY SONG

A DIVINE ADVANTAGE

"Lord, Thou'rt like a wee moosie peepin' oot o' a hole in the wall, for Thou see'st us, but we canna see Thee."

THE REV. MR. HOUSTON

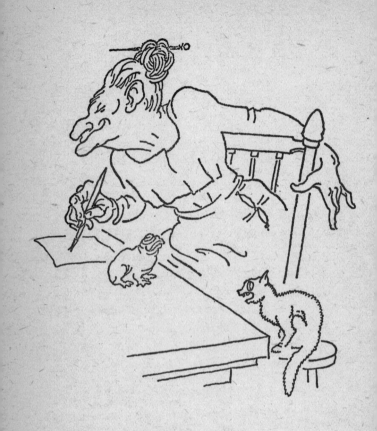

A LETHAL PRAYER

Dean Inge once received a partly anonymous letter
from a lady, who wrote:
> "I am praying for your death. I have been
> very successful in two other instances."

A GRACE FOR LITTLE CHILDREN

Here a little child I stand
Heaving up my either hand;
Cold as paddocks though they be,
Here I lift Them up to Thee,
For a benison to fall
On our meat and on us all.

ROBERT HERRICK

TRADUTTORE, TRADITORE

A missionary, with a very imperfect knowledge of a certain African dialect, translated the benedictory line, "Lord, dismiss us with Thy blessing," so that it read, in native eyes, "Lord, kick us out softly."

A COMMON GRACE

We thank Thee, Lord, for vulgar food,
　　For trotters, tripe, pig's cheek,
For steak and onions, with their crude
　　But appetising reek.

Potatoes in their jackets make
　　Us plain folk honour Thee;
And Thou art with us when we bake
　　Fresh shrimps for Sunday tea.

Thy people's praise is overdue,
　　But see, dear Lord, we kneel
To offer thanks for Irish stew
　　And tasty, cheap cowheel.

Now wait a minute, Lord! Don't miss
　　The last word on our lips:
We thank Thee most of all for this,
　　Thy gift of fish-and-chips.

A. M. L.

AN ANTI-JACOBITE PRAYS

The Whig incumbent of an Edinburgh church did not hesitate to disclose his attitude towards poor Prince Charlie, then holding court at Holyrood: "Bless the King," he prayed. "Thou knowest which King I mean. As for the young man who has come among us to seek an earthly crown, we beseech Thee to take him to Thyself, and bestow on him a crown of glory."

Quoted by ALASDAIR ALPIN MACGREGOR
(in *Auld Reekie: Portrait if a Lowland Boyhood*)

CREATURE COMFORTS

But I, when I undress me,
   Each night upon my knees,
Will pray the Lord to bless me
   With apple-pie and cheese.

ANON. (*American source*)

A GRACE FOR ICE-CREAM

For water-ices, cheap but good,
That find us in a thirsty mood;
For ices made of milk or cream
That slip down smoothly as a dream;
For cornets, sandwiches and pies
That make the gastric juices rise;
For ices bought in little shops
Or at the kerb from him who stops;
For chanting of the sweet refrain:
"Vanilla, strawberry or plain?"
  We thank Thee, Lord, who sendst with heat
  This cool deliciousness to eat.

A. M. L.

A NURSERY LIMERICK

There once was a goose and a wren
Who gave lunch to a cock and a hen:
  "O Lord," prayed the goose,
  "Bless these gifts to our use
And ourselves in Thy service. Amen."

ANON

IN A MONASTERY BEAR-GARDEN

Dean Swift, benighted at an Irish monastery, break-
fasted next morning—a Friday—on bacon and eggs;
but the monks, of course, were having fish. A dis-
play of Irish wit followed, the monks leading off
with the grace: "From bacon and eggs and rotten
legs (Swift was poor on his feet), good Lord deliver
us!" Swift immediately countered with: "From
oysters and cockles and men without bottles, good
Lord deliver us." He followed this up with the lines:

Does any man of common sense
Think ham and eggs give God offence?
Or that a herring has a charm
The Almighty's anger to disarm?
Wrapped in His majesty divine,
D'you think He cares on what we dine?

THE SCOTSMAN'S PRAYER

"O Lord, give us a guid conceit o' oorsel's!"

THE WESSEX PRAYER

God Bless me and me wife,
Me son John and his wife,
Us four:
No more!

POLISHED PIETY

My soul is like a rusty lock:
Lord, oil it with Thy grace;
And rub it, rub it, rub it, Lord,
Until I see Thy face.

OLD PURITAN HYMN

BRIGHT SPARK!

A dissenting minister, at the end of a week of missionary effort, prayed:

"And if any spark of grace has been kindled by these exercises, O, we pray Thee, water that spark!"

THE SOUL-DAY SONG

God bless the Master of this house
    And bless the Missus too
And all the little children
    Around the table, too:
Around the table, true good man,
    And happy may you be,
Sing Father, Son and Holy Ghost
    And life eternally.

A ROYAL METAMORPHOSIS

A presbyterian minister, called on at short notice to officiate at the parish church of Crathie in the presence of Queen Victoria, was so transported by the glory of the occasion that he burst out with the prayer:

"Grant that as she grows to be an old woman she may be made a new man; and that in all righteous causes she may go forth before her people like a he-goat on the mountains."

TAILPIECE

Pray God, by hook or crook,
    Impiety to mend,
And help us, than this book,
    To make a holier end.

                      Amen

MORE
PRAYERS AND GRACES

A CHILD'S PRAYER

Make me, dear Lord, polite and kind
  To everyone, I pray;
And may I ask you how you find
  Yourself, dear Lord, today?

JOHN BANNISTER TABB

A GRUMBLING GRACE

When you got to the table you couldn't go right to eating, but you had to wait for the widow to tuck down her head and grumble a little over the victuals, though there warn't really anything the matter with them.

MARK TWAIN (*Huckleberry Finn*)

SKY PILOT PETITIONED

The heartfelt prayer of a little London girl when she heard a flying-bomb was: "O God, give it strength to go on!"

PRAYER OF A POOR PEDESTRIAN

O God, who filled all heaven with stars
And then all earth with motor cars,
  Make room within thy cosmic plan
  For me, a poor pedestrian.

Spread Thou before me, I entreat,
A threadlike pathway for my feet;
  And do Thou watch me lest I stray
  From this, Thy strait and narrow way.

Give me an ear alert, acute,
For each swift car's peremptory hoot:
  Teach me to judge its headlong pace
  And dodge it with a nimble grace.

When drivers' looks and words are black,
Restrain me, Lord, from answering back:
  O bless me with a nature meek
  To bear with smiles each narrow squeak.

And if one day Thy watchful eye
Should be withdrawn, and I should die,
  One boon I crave, upon my knees:
  Exonerate the driver, please.

A. M. L.

A BULLETIN FOR GOD

We thank Thee, O God, that our friend Joshua Wilkinson is able to sit up and eat a little dry toast...

From a Prayer in a Friends' Meeting House

PIETY AND TURPENTNE

The following petition was sent up by the Rev. Jim McCoy at a prayer meeting in a Georgia turpentine camp:

"O, Lawd, give Thy servant dis mawnin' de eyes ob de eagle an' de wisdom ob de owl; connect his soul wid de gospel telephone in de central skies; 'luminate his brow wid de sun ob Heaven; turpentine his imagination; grease his lips wid possum oil; loosen his tongue wid de sledgehammer ob Thy power; 'lectrify his brain wid de lightnin' ob Thy word; put 'petual motion in his arms; fill him plum full ob de dynamite ob Thy glory; 'noint him all over wid de kerosene ob Thy salvation; and then, deah Lawd, set him on fire."

A PUZZLE FOR OMNIPOTENCE

. . . And be Thou with us and comfort us, O Lord, through eternity—and beyond.

NO VICTORY, NO PRAISE

We desire the Corant-makers to be inspired with the spirit of truth, that one may know when to praise Thy blessed and glorious name and when to pray unto Thee; for we often praise and Laude Thy Holy Name for the King of Sweden's victories and afterwards we heare that there is noe such thing, and we oftentime pray unto Thee to relieve the same King in his distresses, and we Likewise heare that there is noe such Cause.

Prayer offered at the University of
Oxford during the reign of Charles I

A RITUAL COMMENTARY

The Duke of Cambridge, George IV's younger brother, had an amusing, if reprehensible habit of making his own responses to the service in church, aloud. "Let us pray," said the clergyman. "By all means," responded the Duke. On suitable occasions the clergyman would pray for rain. "No good," announced the Duke, after one such prayer, "so long as the wind is in the east."

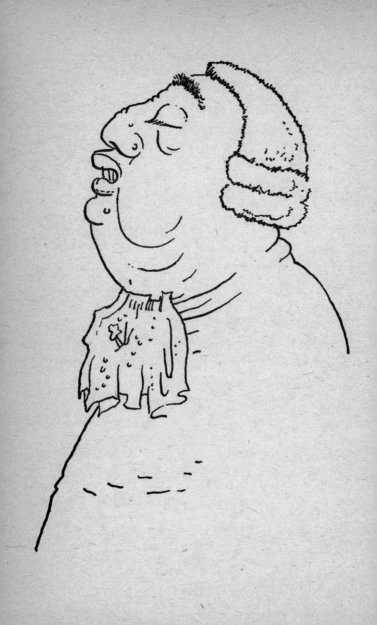

THE LORD AS LAND AGENT

O Lord, Thou knowest that I have nine houses in the city of London, and that I have lately purchased an estate in fee simple in Essex. I beseech Thee to preserve the two counties of Middlesex and Essex from fires and earthquakes. And, as I have also a mortgage in Hertfordshire, I beg Thee also to have an eye of compassion on that county, and for the rest of the counties Thou mayest deal with them as Thou are pleased. O Lord, enable the Banks to answer all their bills, and make all debtors good men. Give prosperous voyage and safe return to the Mermaid sloop because I have not insured it. And because Thou hast said: "The days of the wicked are but short," I trust that Thou wilt not forget Thy promise, as I have an estate in reversion on the death of the profligate young man, Sir J. L. . . . Keep my friends from sinking, preserve me from thieves and housebreakers, and make all my servants so honest and faithful that they may always attend to my interests, and never cheat me out of my property night or day.

Composed by JOHN WARD, M.P., *in 1727*

GOD AND THE PERCYS

A wit who was staying with the Percys found, when
he attended chapel, that the place was so full of
Percy pews, Percy memorials and so forth, that he
wondered the parson did not begin the service with
"Almighty and most Percyful God."

THE LORD'S BUSINESS

(Sir Jacob Astley prays before the Battle of Edgehill)

"O Lord, Thou knowest how busy we must be today: if we forget Thee, do not Thou forget us. For
Christ's sake. Amen."

A COMMINATORY EXERCISE

(*To a sister of an enemy of the author's, who disapproved of "The Playboy of the Western World."*)

Lord, confound this surly sister,
Blight her brow with blotch and blister:
Cramp her larynx, lung and liver:
In her guts a galling give her.

Let her live to eat her dinners
In Mountjoy with seedy sinners:
Lord, this judgment quickly bring,
And I'm your servant, J. M. Synge.

JOHN MILLINGTON SYNGE

A PRAYER FOR ENDURANCE

Lord, on whom all love depends,
Let me make and keep good friends:
Bless me, also, with the patience
To endure my wife's relations.

AMBIGUOUS THANKS

The usual, drastically brief, naval grace is "Thank
God." An admiral, entering late for dinner, looked
round the dining-table and said: "No chaplain?
Thank God."

NUDGING THE LORD

In one of the older Sunday schools, attended by crowds of unruly boys, the Superintendent once prayed:

"O Lord, Jimmy Wilson is leaning head downwards over a form at the back of the room. Grant that he may not fall over and break his neck."

CHROMATIC METABOLISM

On china blue my lobster red
　　Precedes my cutlet brown,
With which my salad green is sped
　　With yellow Chablis down.

Lord, if good living be no sin,
　　But innocent delight,
O polarize these hues within
　　To one eupeptic white!

SIR STEPHEN GASELEE

RELATIVITY

A prayer of the minister of the Cumbrays, two miserable islands in the mouth of the Clyde: "O Lord, bless and be gracious to the Greater and the Lesser Cumbrays and in thy mercy do not forget the adjacent islands of Great Britain and Ireland."

From the DIARY OF SIR WALTER SCOTT

PIOUS BUT PIGHEADED

Grant, O God, that we may always be right, for
Thou knowest we will never change our minds.

OLD SCOTTISH PRAYER

PETITION FROM SAMUEL BUTLER

Searcher of souls, You who in heaven abide,
To whom the secrets of all hearts are open,
Though I do lie to all the world beside,
From me to these no falsehoods shall be spoken.
Cleanse me not, Lord, I say, from secret sin
But from those faults which he who runs can see.
'Tis these that torture me, O Lord, begin
With these and let the hidden vices be;
If You must cleanse these too, at any rate
Deal with the seen sins first, 'tis only reason,
They being so gross, to let the others wait
The leisure of some more convenient season;
    And cleanse not all even then, leave me a few,
    I would not be—not quite—so pure as You.

From the notebooks of SAMUEL BUTLER

IT'S THE INTENTION THAT COUNTS

Little Elsie having been told that Grandma, who was unwell, would be better when the warm weather came, prayed: "God bless Mummy and Daddy, and make it hot for Grandma."

SPOONERIAN WISDOM

The aged and devout rector of a Warwickshire village, wiser than he intended, prayed for "that world which the peace cannot give."

A LAST RESOURCE

Mrs. Kendal, the famous actress, once said to her stage manager: "Bring a kitchen chair and set it in the middle of the stage." She then called for the company and when the company was assembled, she knelt down and prayed: "O Lord, we pray Thee that out of Thy infinite mercy Thou wilt cause some notion of the rudiments of acting to be vouchsafed to this company, for Jesus Christ's sake. Amen." She then got up, dusted her knees and said: "*Well, now, we'll see what that will do!*"

YOU'RE TELLING HIM!

Rufus Jones, of the Society of Friends, was present once at an all-day meeting at which during the closing prayer the minister remembered the omission of several important notices. He prayed: "Thou knowest, O Lord, that there is plenty of lunch for all who may wish to stay at noon, and Thou knowest, O Lord, that there is hay in the shed behind the meeting house for all the horses."

IN SUNDRY PLACES

The guest was late for family prayers, and sat down as he entered, near the door, while his host prayed: "O Lord, before whom all are equal . . ." This prayer finished, and before passing to a reading from the Scriptures, the host signed to his guest to come up and, when he approached, whispered to him: "You are sitting among the servants."

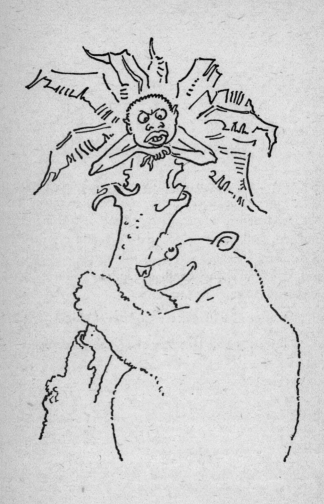

PETITION FOR DIVINE NEUTRALITY

(from a Negro tree'd by a bear)

O Lawd, ef yo' kain't help me, don't help dat b'ar.

SURPRISING GOD

Strange as it may seem to Thee, O God . . .

Beginning of an exordium at a Quaker meeting

THE WRONG ADDRESS

"I am generally so dead beat by the time I kneel down to pray," said the late Henry Hawkins, "that I begin out of habit: 'Gentlemen of the Jury!'"

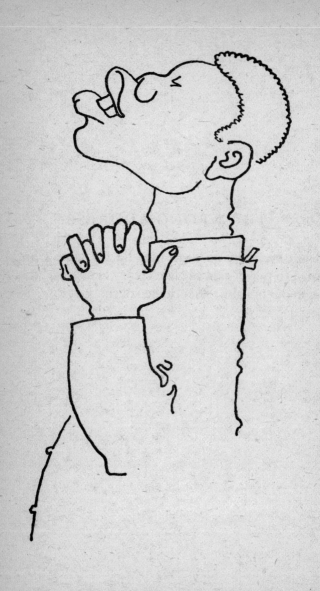

PRINCIPALS ONLY

A negro congregation, praying to Jesus for help in lifting the debt on the church, was interrupted by the pastor, who exclaimed:

"No, Lawd, don' sen' de blessed Jesus. Come right down Yo'self. Dis ain't no boy's job."

THREATENING THE LORD

A certain simple lay-brother in Hemmenrode was very grievously tempted; and once, as he stood in prayer, he used the following words: "Indeed, Lord, if Thou dost not deliver me from this temptation I will complain of Thee to Thy mother." The merciful Lord, who is the master of humility and the lover of simplicity, forestalled the complaint of the lay-brother, as if He feared to be accused to His mother, and immediately made his temptation easier. There was another lay-brother standing behind him at the time, and when he heard this prayer, he smiled and told it to others to edify them.

Who would not be edified by such marvellous humility of the Saviour?

CAESARIUS OF HEISTERBACH

NOT HEAVEN'S TARGET

Lord Londesborough, who was fond of shooting, but a very bad shot, was once heard to exclaim: "O God, You know how much I like shooting. Why won't You allow me to hit these partridges?"

A SPORTING OFFER

The little Negro boy was competing in a race, but kept dropping behind, so that, for a while, his chances of victory seemed slim. Suddenly, however, his legs began to move faster and with great regularity. He passed all his rivals and eventually won the race. Someone asked him afterwards what had happened, and why and what he had been whispering to himself as he ran. He replied that he had been praying to the Lord, saying over and over again: "Lawd, you pick 'em up an' I'll put 'em down."

WHEN THE WORM TURNS

O, may Thy powerful word
   Inspire the feeble worm
To rush into Thy Kingdom, Lord,
   And take it as by storm.

From the Wesleyan Hymnbook

HAPPY AMBIGUITY

At a broadcast of a church service, the minister prayed: "Lord, there are those afflicted by the radio today: comfort them, we ask Thee."

DIVINE CONSULTANT

The deacon of a chapel in Yorkshire, owing to the weight of his years, had been persuaded by the brethren to retire. He agreed, but asked if he might offer a prayer before relinquishing office. He said: "O Lord, if I can no longer be a labourer in your vineyard, will You use me in an advisory capacity?"

INCONGRUOUS ADVICE

F. H. Gillingham, the old Essex cricketer, preaching a sermon in his latter days, implored the old ladies in the congregation "to keep their bats straight and get their left toe out to the pitch of the ball."

ECSTASY OF A BISHOP

An evangelical bishop, watching a football match, sees the centre-forward slam the ball into the net. He thereupon throws his silk hat into the air, crying: "Oh, what an abundantly blessed goal!"

THE CROFTER'S PRAYER

A crofter, holding family prayers on a Sabbath night, offered prayer for his three sons, William, a soldier, John, in the Royal Navy, and Davie, aged seventeen, living at home and helping on the croft:

O Lord God of Battles, stretch forth Thy hand, we beseech Thee, over oor Wullie, who, as Thou art aware, is a sodger, in the Seaforth Highlanders, and is fechtin' in France. Protect him from all the perils o' the battlefield, and bring him hame safe after a victorious peace. And O Lord, Thou whose paths are in the sea, and whose ways are in the deep watters, stretch forth Thy protecting hand over oor John, a Leading Seaman in the Royal Sovereign: guard him from all the perils of the sea and guide him hame in safety unto the harbour where he would be.

An' then, Lord, there's wee Davie—ach, Lord, never fash yer thoomb aboot wee Davie. He's here at hame wi' us, and we can look after him wursels.

PRAYER OF A PROPERTY
PROFITEER

On Sunday, Lord, a Mrs. Drew
Is coming here the house to view
    Which is, of course, for sale.
Grant Thou, O Lord, that she forbear
From standing long upon the stair
    That is, alas! too frail.

O do not let her hand draw back
The curtain and reveal the crack
    Along the window-pane!
O guide her as she comes and goes,
So that no smell assails her nose
    From the adjacent drain.

Let her not see the neighbouring slum
As she approaches. May she come
    Along the better road,
And grant that she may, in a trice,
Agree to the inflated price
    We ask for our abode.

And grant, O Lord, to us who plead,
These favours that we may succeed
    In what we now devise,
And through thine all-embracing love
Be made eternal tenants of
    Thy mansion in the skies.

HARLEY QUINN

THE LORD IS MISINFORMED

I observe that in the form of prayer for use on January 3 we are to ask forgiveness "because we have indulged in national arrogance, finding satisfaction in our power over others rather than in our ability to serve them." May I point out that this is a severe censure on all public servants in India, the Crown Colonies, and the Mandated Territories? What grounds are there for stating that this large body of public servants have grossly failed in their duty?

From a letter to "The Times"

GRACE BEFORE MEAT

O Lord, when hunger pinches sore,
    Do thou stand us in stead,
And send us from thy bounteous store
    A tup- or wether-head!

ROBERT BURNS

GRACE AFTER MEAT

Lord, Thee we thank and Thee alone,
    For temporal gifts we little merit;
At present we will ask no more—
    Let William Hislop bring the spirit.

ROBERT BURNS